By Herself

Also by Debora Greger

Movable Islands (1980)

And (1985)

The 1002nd Night (1990)

Off-Season at the Edge of the World (1994)

Desert Fathers, Uranium Daughters (1996)

God (2001)

Western Art (2004)

Men, Women, and Ghosts (2008)

By Herself

Debora Greger

PENGUIN POETS

PENGUIN BOOKS
Published by the Penguin Group
Penguin Group (USA) Inc., 375 Hudson Street, New York, New York 10014, U.S.A.
Penguin Group (Canada), 90 Eglinton Avenue East, Suite 700, Toronto, Ontario, Canada M4P 2Y3
(a division of Pearson Penguin Canada Inc.)
Penguin Books Ltd, 80 Strand, London WC2R 0RL, England
Penguin Ireland, 25 St Stephen's Green, Dublin 2, Ireland (a division of Penguin Books Ltd)
Penguin Group (Australia), 250 Camberwell Road, Camberwell, Victoria 3124, Australia
(a division of Pearson Australia Group Pty Ltd)
Penguin Books India Pvt Ltd, 11 Community Centre, Panchsheel Park, New Delhi - 110 017, India
Penguin Group (NZ), 67 Apollo Drive, Rosedale, Auckland 0632, New Zealand
(a division of Pearson New Zealand Ltd)
Penguin Books (South Africa) (Pty) Ltd, 24 Sturdee Avenue, Rosebank, Johannesburg 2196,
South Africa

Penguin Books Ltd, Registered Offices:
80 Strand, London WC2R 0RL, England

First published in Penguin Books 2012

10 9 8 7 6 5 4 3 2 1

LIBRARY OF CONGRESS CATALOGING IN PUBLICATION DATA
Greger, Debora, 1949–
   By herself / Debora Greger.
      p. cm.—(Penguin Poets)
   Poems.
   ISBN 978-0-14-312239-5
   I. Title.
   PS3557.R42B9 2012
   811'.54—dc23
                              2012023587

Printed in the United States of America
Set in Granjon LT Std
Designed by Sabrina Bowers

*for my father
and in memory of my mother*

Contents

III

IV

my foreword to silence,
my psalm turned inside out.

—TOMAS TRANSTRÖMER

I

Who are the great forgetters
Who will know just how to make us forget such and such a part of
    the world
Where is the Christopher Columbus to whom is owed the forgetting
    of a continent

—APOLLINAIRE

The Vacant Lot at the End of the Street

I. Death Takes a Holiday

In a suit woven of the finest mist,
Death took the last seat on the train,

the one next to me. He loosened his tie.
His cell phone had nothing to say to him

as he gazed out the window, ignoring us all.
Had England changed since he was last

on holiday here, a hundred years ago?
Like family, rather than look at each other,

we watched the remains of empire smear the glass.
Had we met somewhere? "Out West last week,

I passed your parents' house," he said.
"I waved but your mother didn't notice.

Your father must have turned off his hearing aid,
in that way he has." In the rack overhead,

a net, a jar, a box, a pin: Death had come
for another British butterfly.

He rose, unwrinkled. "I'll see you later," he said.

II. Demeter in Winter

Earlier and earlier, the dark
comes to the door, but no one knocks.

No, the wind scratches at the window.
Clouds skate the ice of your old room.

Daughter, a cloud falls to the floor
and can't get up—

or are you my sister? Remember the rope
tied from schoolhouse to home,

so the blizzard could find its way to us?
It climbed into the attic,

spread a white sheet, and invited us to hibernate.
Who left behind the army greatcoat

into whose cave we crawled that night?
Lie down beside me. Under a blanket of snow,

something freezes: the mind's gray rag,
caught on a rusty nail. Come closer.

Say I am not the woman I used to be,
just bones turned to sand in a sack of skin.

Daughter, if this page isn't blank, turn to the next
and read me the part where you disappear.

III. Persephone on the Way to Hell

Over there, beside the road—
is that the letter I should have left you, Mother?
The shade of a scarecrow waves a blank page
as big as he is.

Blond waves of winter wheat roll up
to the knees he'll never have,
tempting his shirt to set sail
for some other myth.

He's a white plastic bag
tied to a stake and stuck in a field
at the end of summer. What's left of a river
shrinks from a bed grown too big for it,

surrounded by rocks it carried this far.
Mother seemed smaller, too.
I saw how you, my lord of the dark,
took her hand as if it were a child's.

"Where am I?" she wanted to know,
reigning from her old recliner. You knelt
and took off her shoes.
In her mind, a door closed by itself.

IV. The River of Forgetting

"Why aren't you packed to leave town?"
my mother asked. Why was I holding a rock
worn down until smooth,
gone dull when it dried?

Where were we? She prided herself
on being born with no sense of direction,
so where were the fifty years
of maps my father drew for her?

Did she remember her own name at the end?
Remember for her, you modest house,
so like the others that only those
who die there can tell them apart.

Cottonwoods crowding the driveway,
did your leaves whisper which turn
the dead should take to the water?
The ferry that hasn't run for decades

leaves for the river of forgetting tonight.

V. The Azalea Justifies Its Existence

Dream of yourself or stay awake,
Martial says, and the azalea agrees.
Fifty weeks it dreams,

not the greater green of Florida
the rest of us do, but a pink almost red,
a shade forgotten for thirty years:

a coat marked down, and down again;
coat in a color not from the desert
of subtleties my mother favored

but somewhere between magenta and mauve—
but a coat in her size, and so she bought it.
Finding her in a crowd, you found yourself

facing spring come before its time.
Yesterday she died.
She couldn't lift a spoon

to the watery winter light of the Great Basin.
Azalea, if she could see you, ruddled with rust.
You some ridiculously ruffled thing

thrown on in a rush to condole.
Petal so far beyond the pink of *flushed* and *fevered*
you're—what is the word for such ragged,

joy-riddled gauds of grief?

VI. The Death of Demeter

From a distance, a woman's life is nothing
but a glass of ice water losing its edge.

I should know, Daughter. I spent the night
in a graveyard, behind a tombstone,

trying to stay cold. The trees
that wouldn't stop sighing—

they're nothing but chairs and tables
dying not to become tables and chairs.

A tree cries out to be covered with leaves?
A deep breath of dirt fills the lungs.

Permit me to propose a few things.
I don't want my soul to find its body.

VII. The School for the Dead

The blackboard's endless night,
a constellation of chalk dust unnamed—

through the classroom window, I saw a map
pulled down like a window shade:

continents pushed apart an ocean
blotting out names with tears.

South America and Africa no longer nestled
like spoons in a silver drawer.

The lost mitten of Greenland froze
to the Arctic Circle, the empty space

called Canada yawned. The new pupil,
my mother, hunched in a desk too small,

waiting for her daughter the professor
to begin the obedience lesson:

how to lie down. How to roll over
in the grave. How to play dead.

VIII. Nocturne for Female Voice

I walk the old street at night, the way I always did.
Daughter, why didn't you come?
I had to talk to a tree. I talked to dogs—
they bark at anything, even a ghost.

You shiver, but know nothing of the cold.
Cheatgrass spares the ashen its barbs,
Night shrouds me in darkness,
wind wraps me in dirt—where's *your* coat?

You've been to Rome with a man
you weren't married to, and now you know ruins?
If the body is a temple,
as the nuns tried to teach you long ago,

it collapses on itself, bringing down the mind.
The vacant lot at the end of your childhood—
which of us rules it now? I lower myself
to the puncture vine, the weed

I warned you never to step on. I prostrate myself,
the way you coax something to grow in arid land.
Here's a pale star that blooms a week
and then bears a fruit, pure thorn.

It survives by causing pain.
I walk our street at night, the way I always did.
Why didn't you come? I had to bark at a tree.
I howled like a dog.

IX. In the Library of the Dead

I closed the book I hadn't read.
Who wanted for food
when you could smuggle something

snatched from the jaws of the vending machine
into the library of the dead?
Down on my shoulder came a hand:

my late mother's, turned to ash.
In the house where she died,
we would sit, not speaking,

for another eternity: she had her book
and pressed one upon me, companionably.
Everything had shrunk

to fit in a suitcase when I left.
The past had been ironed flat,
a thousand leaves starched and pinned

to a cottonwood just a shade of its former self,
the only sound its rustle, industrious,
leaves turning waxen, unread—

though no shelf lay empty
in the library of the dead.

To a Spoonbill

I

What was left of the lake,
the osprey felt, were the fish
too small to bother with:
you scratched the surface

and came up empty-clawed.
From a bald cypress, you sulked.
Alligators walked on water
they could no longer swim;

they tiptoed in their expensive shoes,
hungry enough to eat one another.
The lake had been this low before,
said a beer can spitting sand

onto the new expanse of shore.
A fishing lure dangled from a weed,
a spangle trying to catch a bird's eye.
Some fisherman had pinned

a corsage of tangled line to a dead reed.
Farther down, past a rotting log,
a scrap of something pink
wavered, too pink, in the heavy air.

In all this death, how could that be?
At the outer limits of my binoculars,
I unriddled a blush of tutu,
a beak of two wooden spoons.

My first roseate spoonbill,
you're too far north. Are you ugly or beautiful?
Your commedia dell'arte bill
sieves the shallows for a taste of mud.

O my unlikely one!
Where would you *not* look out of place?
You won't let me draw any closer,
I the one who doesn't belong.

II

Do you see someone back there,
not girl, not woman, disguised as a bird?
In the school cafeteria, as in a bad dream,
watery music trickled from a tape recorder

built like a boulder left behind by a river.
In satin and tulle, in scuffed ballet slippers,
I stood on a raft made of tables
as if adrift on the radioactive Columbia River.

O talent show in the desert of memory!
Each night an old costume, grown too small,
claims it knew me when we were young.
Must I go on? Swept downstream,

notes wobbled and ripped. My sister—
how had she crossed the stage and vanished
into the shallows of folding chairs
where nuclear chemists clapped?

O Father-Daughter Banquet!
O Tchaikovsky, O chicken Kiev!
What did those men wish for us?
Not the life of an artiste. Not even

Seattle, just over the mountains.
They held out the postwar promise
of fatherly warmth: cheap nuclear power.
They would keep the Sahara of childhood

safe for its daughters, ragweed and sandbur.
Into the mud of middle age, I step,
bones empty as flutes. Fly away,
spoonbill, fly away home.

After the Fall: Eve in Florida

How long had I stood by a lake drying up?
Something cracked twenty feet above me,

as if an angel had stepped on a branch
that wouldn't bear such weight.

Something crashed through leaves—
not a branch but a snake come down

to my level. It lay where it had fallen,
stunning me, too. What did it want this time?

Nothing but my shadow,
where it unrolled a long gold stripe.

Fallen one, bare your fangs.
Once I opened mine and ate.

Who's holy now? We shrug another skin.
And still, in the parking lot at the edge

of paradise, time weighed itself down,
fattened with salt, with rain unshed.

Domestic Manners of the Americans

I. In the Pasture

In the university pasture,
sunlight raked the dew around a few cattle.
Sandhill cranes, in town
for the winter, poked the ground

and one another,
strutted, flapped and flounced,
and from fierce beaks
let loose a rattle part water, part wood.

Then they seemed smaller,
no longer silvery. Above all this,
keeping their company,
never lifting his voice, there being no other

of his kind to call,
loomed a bird so rare I never thought
I'd see it, except on paper:
the tallest in North America.

Far from the fence,
almost to the trees that hide the houses
crowding a last open space—
a whooping crane.

II. In the Trees at the Alligator Farm

Like hats in a shop window, left over
          from the lost age
of millinery, egrets were nesting.
          Males fanned plumes

to impress a female. I was impressed
          by how she clung
to a branch as he leapt to her back,
          the tree almost

brought to its knees. But, at its crown,
          a rectory of wood storks
refused to be shaken. Their woody beaks
          clacked antediluvian approval.

A flock of male photographers staggered by,
          each lens longer
than the one before, all pointed—
          two eggs mocked

the color of sky reflected in the weedy water.
          Part lint, part craw,
a nestling waited for its silky mother
          to land, to lower

the long rope of her slender neck
          and, in dainty waves,
regurgitate the rich black bile
          of family happiness.

Night School in Florida

In the middle of class, I started longing
for something greener than the word "green,"
wilder than "wild."

The moon the dead poets favored
rose over the parking lot of the present,
looking for a graveyard to hang itself above.

Glaring at us with the pudgy face
of our classroom bully, the clock
that rapped its hand, hard, for silence,

the moon—I need another word for "moon."
On the dark side of the planet School,
where the word "cloud" had been erased,

leaving a cloud-shaped smudge,
some lunar chalk dust whirled.
Shadows ran the other way.

And there, on the window, something
was watching us: a green tree frog.
By which I mean "viridescent." Or "verdurous."

I mean grassy, leafy, mossy—I can only mean *green*.
Skin smooth, enameled by Fabergé,
the frog waited for a moth

to be drawn to our false, fluorescent light.
Only in the dark would it sing,
a quaint, cowbell-like *quaink*.

The night would flood with a campanology
so green you'd think of handbells.
Of the way, after you shake one

to make it speak, you have to hold it
to your chest to still the overtones,
hard against the quake

of your inconsequential heart.

The Unicorn of Florida

Sir John Hawkins, 1564

I

The natives wear bits of horn about their necks
and affirm they derive from a beast that,
coming to the river to drink,

puts its singular horn to the water first.
Men of our company have procured some pieces
at negligible expense, as have the French:

enough so that it must be supposed
there *are* unicorns—which, for want of time and people,
have not been found. I trust God

will reveal their whereabouts before long,
to the great profit of those who hunt them down.
Of beasts in this country,

besides deer, fox, hare, polecat, leopard,
and the native peoples, I am unable to say;
but it is thought there be lion and tiger as well.

Of the enmity between lion and unicorn,
we have been continually informed.
There is no beast but has his foe:

the sheep, the wolf; the elephant, the rhinoceros;
the king, his lords—nay, other kings;
and so on. Where a lion reigns,

the unicorn cannot be missing.

II

The captain saw a serpent with three heads
and four feet, the size of a spaniel,
which, for want of a harquebus,

he dared not attempt to slay.
There are, as well, fish the size of smelt
to be seen flying along the coast.

Upon land and sea, there are many fowl;
but on land I, your Adam, was unable to name any,
my abode was so short. On fresh rivers,

these two be chief: the Flemengo
having red feathers, and long red legs like a heron,
and an egret white as the swan,

that has in her tail feathers
so fine a plume it surpasses the ostrich.
All the year long, this place is the green of Eden,

which is to say, of summer in England.
Once a day, without fail, they receive a shower
from above. If not for the want of gold,

foretold in abundance—the very thing we have,
to our cost, daily endeavored to find—
this would have been Paradise

a moment before the Fall, or just after.

My First Mermaid

In Florida, where these things can happen,
we stopped at the last roadside attraction.

In a small theater decorated with mold,
behind a curtain sagging like seaweed,

a wall of glass held back a wall of water.
And there, in the springs, a woman in a bikini top

and Lycra fish tail held an air hose to her lips
like a microphone. What was she waiting for?

Into the great open bowl of the springs
a few fish drifted. They looked at the two of us.

They shook their heads and their bodies rippled.
Air bubbles shimmered in the filtered sun,

each silver *O* racing to the surface to break.
We'd missed the day an unscripted underwater blimp

of a manatee wobbled into view. The gray, whiskered lard
of a sea cow or the young woman who sang—

lip-synched, rather—some forgettable song,
her lipstick waterproof: which was the real mermaid?

II

Given the weight of water, nothing happens fast
to a mermaid, whether it's love or loss.

Not like the landlocked life, I wanted to warn her.
But here came a prince in street clothes,

trying to think thoughts that were heavy enough
to make himself sink to her level. His shirt ballooned,

a man turned not to a merman but a manatee.
Yet, in the small eternity it took for him

to grasp her greasy flipper, for her to find
his more awkward human ankle, and then

for them to turn, head over each other's heels—
a ring rolling away, too beautiful to catch—

they lived happily ever after.
Until one of them had to stop for breath.

The Nightingale of Florida

Night fell on the rain, rain on the dark.
Cloud gauzed the moon.
Drowsily, a greenhouse frog chirped,
as if, in dream, something took wing.
How many years did I, new to this state,
think a frog's call a bird's?

A leaf not quite heart-shaped shook.
Through the small hour, half in love
with places he wouldn't live to see,
half with death, the sodden shade
of Keats wandered. Half my age—no, less.
Sit, ghost, and let me read to you

of a large frog whose grunt resembles that of swine.
There is a frog that sounds like a loud cowbell:
one begins, another answers, the sound passed round,
rising and sinking, depending how the wind of evening sits.
The noisiest is the shad frog. You would be persuaded
men assembled in serious debate where there are none.

Oh, for a beaker full of the warm South.
Set one outside to fill with rain
for the poet who was always cold.
Darkling, listen to the greenhouse frog
pour forth something like an ode to sleep,
the one you didn't live to start.

In rainwater, I write your name.

At the House of the Dead

I. The Cadillac

didn't want to come back to life.
Next door, the dead man's son
tried to persuade the car to cough.

Maps folded flat as gloves,
stacked in the glove compartment—
what was the best route to the next world?

There was still gas in the tank,
but the big white boat of a thing
sat in the driveway like a Viking ship,

waiting for burial. Some great age, lost,
and then another, had passed this house by,
until it was owned by the swifts

that nested in the chimney. For them,
nothing had changed—or else some silence,
no longer human, had been perfected.

No longer did the dead man's violin protest
his trying to teach it to speak,
if not to sing. O violet evenings!

Now the only chatter that rose
was the birds', dark wings outspread
to catch the last of the light.

Then back they fell into their deeper dark.
All night they clung to its steep sides
in sleep, as death clings to life.

II. Bindweed

clambers over the hedge.
Flaring its lips, it opens a purple throat.
Rose-pink bells roar. But, as in sleep

when you open your mouth
to call to someone about to leave,
no sound comes out, not even a whisper.

There is nothing to say.
Bindweed has taken over the hedge
at our neighbor the dead man's house.

He would not have allowed it,
or the stubby fans of palmetto
rushing back for an encore.

But now the mockingbird on the porch
mocks the ring of a phone. Good neighbors,
the bells of bindweed keep their distance

from one another along the vine.
Someone has creased the leaves
into careless dark cards of condolence.

A Short Pause in the Requiem

On the edge of town, a stillness so raw
I don't recognize it
builds a cathedral to the body,
not the soul.

In the subtropics of Lent,
down the valley of each leaf
rolls an acidic tear.
Spring peepers,

has this brand-new church
left you a little swamp at the edge
of its vast and pious parking lot?
You stop to draw breath

in order to go on singing, louder,
even sadder. Insects that fly too close
to your quick tongues—
what would they have us mourn?

Let there be waters enough to hide you
from herons on the hunt.
Let there be *rainy rainy rainy rain,*
as you say. Let there come

someone to build us an *ark ark ark.*

Still Life with Hurricane

We readied the house.
We showed the hurricane
how we'd bought enough water
to make a small lake.

"So, no need to fill the bathtub," I said.
The hurricane sighed,
"What happened to the girl
who grew up in a sandstorm?

What's the use of bringing the beach
all the way to her house, grain by grain?
Why lay the ghost quartz of Florida at her feet?
The desert must be inside her now."

So the storm pounded feathery fists
at the door of the sweet gum tree.
Where was the wren that knew
the seedy wallpaper of its rooms?

With barely a groan, the tree gave up
its biggest branch. Did the crash come first,
or the leaf-shudder? Gray flags
of Spanish moss tattered in the gale.

Hurricane, you've taken the power.
Do you want the porch swing, too?
A small ghost sits there, refusing to come in.
Hurricane, shake her again.

II

There can't any poet come out here and sit on the shaky rail of our ugly bridges and sing us into paradise.

—SHERWOOD ANDERSON

Once I came to paradise. It was empty.

—HARRY MARTINSON

After the Hurricane

the ant leaned into a grain of sand,
pushing it toward the light

the way, in the dream, I tried to lift a column
of air off of my chest. When had I sunk to the porch?

I couldn't lift even my eyelids,
though I sensed I was at the wrong house.

My mother the wind had moved out,
taking the rain, leaving a mess.

I turned my back to it. I stretched out
beside a sweet gum branch that had pruned itself,

and listened: water slid down the drip-tip
of every leaf on this corner of earth.

Who was happy now? A tree frog barked
to celebrate a world made wet. In the gloom,

another called the world to sleep.
One rang a bell, one plucked a string.

By the cracked swimming pool across the street,
frogs adjusted the pitch of their trills

until they braided a stream that wandered
deeper into sleep. There you found me

by putting up walls so you could open a door.

In the Heart of England

Down the aisle
of some dim cathedral, the dark ran ahead.
My sandals clattered,

doing their part to wear away the dates
chiseled in stone.
Whose gnawed bones lay down below?

England, I'm not dressed
warmly enough for my past, let alone for yours,
both gone so cold.

Where was the woman who stood here
twenty years ago?
I'd worn away like the lady carved in gray

on this tomb. At her side,
under chain mail gouged, link by stony link,
a knight surrendered,

to the rot that underlay eternal rest.
How many men
did he kill in the name of king or god?

Joined in prayer,
his hands shaped a spire—or was it a blade?
He warmed his feet

on a faithful dog, barely touching
the wife beside him.
The folds of her gown had eroded,

as if smoothed
by a waiting hand, again and then again,
she having died first,
by years.

Chekhov in English

Tea by lamplight
and then Mother, the artist,
drifted upstairs with the visiting poet

in search of a word.
Father, ex-sergeant, veteran
of Cyprus, Aden, and Belfast,

who'd seen the empire
crumble like cake, retired
to the piano. Through a dainty minefield

of dances, he tiptoed:
the *English Suites* of Bach,
who never cared to invade these isles.

The eldest son,
a gardener, had fallen asleep.
The armchair sagged under the weight

of the season gardeners hate—
not the cold or the dark but the leaves,
notes still falling, the movement never over.

Scraps of paper fell
at my feet, a clumsy snow:
I, the guest, cut out a paper donkey.

I cut off its tail
for the grown daughter
who didn't know what to do with her life

except to plan a party
at a home where the aged went
when they turned into children again.

O dead of winter!
The isle leaned into the dark.
Winds from Siberia crossed the North Sea

to knock at the door.
I opened it: the street was blue.
Across the way, a living room glowed,

curtains undrawn,
a stage set lacking actors.
And now they entered. I could see

their lips move
out of love and cruelty
the way that happy families' do.

Dream with Basement

I'm back, in the dream, and looking around.
I know that backyard. To this rocky place,
my father loved bringing more:

chunks of the finest obsidian from Oregon
poke their sharp little beaks out of apple boxes
into the cutting air of Washington.

The cardboard sags at the thought
of even the smallest rain ever falling.
It's too hot to long for a cloud

and hit one rock with another until it breaks—
but that's the way you start an arrowhead,
if you're my father, down in the basement.

Upstairs, the Iron Age is heating up.
Can you smell things burning in a dream?
From where I stand on the basement stairs,

I sense my mother's forging leftovers into lunch.
How little I know myself compared to this landing
between one vanished age and another.

Broom, you've lost your thick shock of hair,
just like my father. Dustpan, remember
what I broke? No one else knows.

Dances of 1964

What was family for, if not to retreat from?
I closed the door of my bedroom.

I was almost fifteen, intent on hiding
a scrap of sadness I refused to share.

And a grown-up taste, almost sweet,
like dust the wind delivered with love,

or something worse, to every room,
no matter how hermitic the seal.

In that small town of nuclear engineers,
in the plain government-issue mirror,

I saw a stranger, neither girl nor woman.
She'd made herself ill enough to stay home

rather than learn to do the fox-trot.
Oh, 1914, was that you, back from the dead

to teach me what you called the latest craze?
Let the boys of third-period gym,

draft cards in their wallets, trip over the gunboats
of their own feet. Under breath yet unsoured,

let them count the steps our grandfathers memorized
on the way to the trenches.

Hands clammy as a boy's—maybe I *was* sick.
The narrow bed had room for one,

so Sadness made me bear its weight.
How long did it take to turn to stone?

I longed to be crushed until hard
as a diamond waiting to be cut or loved.

And then came a cry from afar:
the teenage anchorite called to lunch.

Scratching at the window with a branch
of the cottonwood—tell me, Subtraction

and Long Division, are you there,
you the ones who held me first?

West of Myself

Why are you still seventeen
and drifting like a dog after dark,
dragging a shadow you've found?

Put it back where it belongs,
and that bend of river, too. That's not the road
you want, though you have it to yourself.

Gone are the cars that crawl to town
from the reactors, a parade of insects, metallic,
fuming along the one four-lane street.

The poplars of the shelterbelt lean away
from the bypass that never had much to pass by
but coyote and rabbitbrush.

Pinpricks stabbed in a map too dark to read—
I stared at stars light-years away.
Listen. That hissing? Just a sprinkler

damping down yesterday until it's today.
The cottonwoods shiver, or I do,
every leaf rustling as if it's the one

about to tear itself away, not I.
Memory takes the graveyard shift.

The Ruins of Childhood

So this is how Sleeping Beauty felt when she woke.
Only the rivers are heavier, the miles longer.

I can't see the burial garden for nuclear submarines,
just the new cemetery, the one patch of green.

How long have I been away? Not that long,
if you count the dreams. But I don't know the names

of the new streets rolled like ribbons in the dirt.
New house, you bear a rattlesnake's old address.

How sad, the old Westgate strip of shops,
name and all. O western gate to nothing much,

then or now! Let us praise the poet who,
from the ridge of the Pei-mang Hills,

looked down on a city lost eighteen centuries ago:
In Lo-yang how still it is!

I think of the house I lived in all those years:
Heart-tied, I cannot speak.

Preserves

The past is closed today,
but you may look in the windows—
though the house where you grew up stands empty.
On this perfect Gobi of a morning,

your father put on his dosimeter and went off to work.
Everyone else is in the backyard,
at a picnic table covered with newspaper,
bottling whatever can be preserved.

And there you are, the eldest child,
hand still so small you're the only one
who can pack the slumped fruits of summer
into the narrow-mouthed jar of winter.

It's the beautiful thing about you.
The pinkish blood of a blanched tomato
drips down your arm, stinging as it goes,
yesterday's headlines blurring where it falls.

Some August, late in the age of black and white—
I can just make out a shot of the president
and his younger brother. Who's in the background
in a dark suit? Is that you, Death?

How young they look, never to grow old.

Not Thinking About the Past

In an idle hour I thought of former days;
And former friends seemed to be standing in the room.

—PO CHÜ-I, "THINKING OF THE PAST," 833 CE

Pebbles of rain dashed against the window,
the old days begging to be let in—
and then what shade lay beside me?

Whose hand was cool under my blouse?
The dark was a cave, the cave a boy's mouth,
my tongue a blind snake feeling its way in—

or was the way out what I sought?
The past is a cave carved in the rain.
And where is that boy who became nothing to me?

He left town a marijuana dealer
and came back a librarian, or so I heard.
How long has he lain in the ground, refusing to age?

I heard he willed his record collection
to the library he stole it from.
The dull needle of the past drags in a dark groove.

Through the undergrowth of hisses and scratches
that filled those old records with time,
a voice courses like a stream

that ferries some mountain of loss,
grain by grain, to the salt of the sea.
Into a clearing in Gluck's opera

a woman in powdered wig and breeches steps,
claiming she's a man named Orpheus.
Even with his mouth full of sand,

he can sing the dead back to life.
He can bring a rock to tears.

Guide to the Dark

Late, too late, walking alone,
I stepped on a shadow that wasn't mine:

my older brother had climbed out of his grave
after fifty years, to see me home.

A black dog chained to a blacker tree
shook the night by the scruff but raised no voice.

The moon turned its face away, into a cloud.
Dead before I was born, never photographed,

not even a name written once in a Bible, a blotch—
how light he was, this stranger I'd never met.

I could see through him to a deeper dark,
mud sewn shut by a pale family of roots.

What did he want? He couldn't say.
What could I offer him? Even less. Underfoot,

I crushed a leaf whose name I couldn't remember
and up rose the sweet, sickly scent of mortification.

Yes

Yes, your childhood now a legend of fountains

—JORGE GUILLÉN

Yes, your childhood, now a legend
gone to weeds, still remembers the gray road
that set out to cross the desert of the future.

And how, always just ahead,
gray water glittered, happy to be just a mirage.
Who steps off the gray bus at the depot?

Sidewalks shudder all the way home.
Blinds close their scratchy eyes.
Who settles in your old room?

Stuffy air sprawls as if it owns the place,
and now your teenage secrets have no one to tell.
For the spider laying claim to the corner,

there is a stickiness to spin, that the living may beg
to be wrapped in silk and devoured,
leaving not even the flinch from memory.

Too Close

Love, I haven't met you yet. I'm out the door,
late for a bus, suitcase spilling open,
disgorging my life so far.

I won't be needing it, but I don't know that yet.
Bus driver, go slowly around the bends
of dream so as not to wake me.

But don't fall asleep yourself, no matter how flat
a girl's landscape seems.
I rub the pillow of the window

with my sleeve and look myself in the eye,
my cheek sutured by a fence
keeping emptiness off the empty road.

Yesterday takes forever to cross
and then the day before that.
Bus driver, don't drive so near the river—

or is that an irrigation ditch?
Is that thunder I hear, or engine trouble?
It never rains in the past.

Love, am I on my way to you?
It will take years of nights like this
for me to arrive.

III

I cross
the street that's followed me so long

—TOMAS TRANSTRÖMER

The Clock in the Heart

in memory of Victoria Moore, 1961–2005

I

The clock in the heart of town
missed the courthouse torn down long ago.

The clock suffered itself to be wound,
then told some other time. What was the rush?

The train was late, as always,
the train that no longer ran from ocean to gulf.

Gone were the flatbeds stacked with logs,
the boxcars of pencils from Cedar Key.

Still, the depot stood, shuttered,
a puffed-up pigeon now stationmaster.

A cloud crossed the platform—
was it you, V., as you were twenty years ago,

come to college with your grandmother's Samsonite?
My first student, let me carry your suitcase.

You won't need that heavy coat
or the grassy blanket, the bedsheet of dirt.

No one dies, then comes to Florida—
no, just the reverse.

II

They plugged your ears with cotton
and folded your hands, not to be opened again.

A silky pillow was plumped for your bald head.
Some chemical formed a bead

at the tip of a syringe: a pearl the size of the soul,
if there were such a thing. Leave us.

The River Styx lies south of here, in the next county,
you'll recall. Don't chase a kingfisher across it.

If you need to rest, don't crawl into a hole
in the bank, the way the swallows do.

Fold your wings in the weeds that flourish
by Elysian Fields, the new "golf retirement community."

Hawks hunt the living on one side of the river;
vultures shadow the dead on the other. Stay low.

The Middle of Nowhere

Some small hour grew even smaller.
    In the middle of nowhere,
      the bus turned
    from the frayed ribbon of road
toward a patch of street, where a sketch

of a water tower stretched out in sleep.
    Was that tall, dark mass
      at the end of the block
    a grain elevator or a volume missing
from a vast encyclopedia of emptiness?

We pulled into what passed for a depot
    in what was barely a town:
      the one filling station.
    A bathtub stood on stout legs
in the ladies' room, ready to bathe the family

who owned the business. They must have lived
    somewhere in the back, because,
      even at that hour,
    a child flitted like a moth
into the light that spread like an oil slick

around the pumps. A woman shook her head—
    at the kid or the driver, it was far
      from clear. In limbo,
    what was one more night
where no one arrived, let alone departed?

A Short History of the West

John Singer Sargent, in the Rockies, 1916

It was always raining or snowing.
My tent flooded, mushrooms sprouted in my boots,
porcupines took shelter in my clothes.
Canned food always fried in a black frying pan
got on my nerves, and the only attraction
to the place, a fine waterfall, thundered all night.
I stood it for three weeks, coming away

with a repulsive painting.
Then the weather changed,
and I am off to try the simple life again
in a tent at the top of another valley,
this time with gridiron instead of frying pan,
and a perforated rubber mat to stand on.
It takes time to learn how to be really happy.

Life was different in Montana.
Why didn't I stay there? We toured new trails
each day; Mrs. Livermore was perfectly delightful
and played chess. Alas, she went east
and struck Chicago in the heat.
The refrigerated dining room
at the Blackstone saved her life,

as it had mine two weeks before.
It is worth heading there from anywhere
in America during a heat wave. You sit
in perfect temperatures over an excellent meal
and watch the crowd outside the window
dying like flies. Nero could not improve on it.

Bitterness

I don't even know whom this bitterness is for.

—VALLEJO

Air so clear, it made you look away—
I recognized a blue I'd seen only once before,
on the ceiling of a church I'd stepped into
somewhere in Italy: pure ultramarine,
the most expensive grade.

Beneath such sky,
how could the heart not aspire to dryness?
The Arizona air clarified everything:
shade had never been so sharp.
You could cut yourself on it,

yet I longed to be taken in.
I reached out to touch, not my beloved,
but a cactus—I don't know why.
It seemed so near, I reached for a mountain peak
as if to test the blade of a knife.

The slopes were blushing: you were dying,
sun. Again. Theatrically,
you hung my little medal of pain
on your chest, waiting for it to melt.
You flung yourself down one last valley.

What good the sad twists of the one road up?
Let moon and coyote fight over it.
The road turned blue. The dry wash barked.
Where was the coldness of love,
called "water" in those parts?

For whom was that bitterness meant?
I don't know. But I drank.

One Sunday Out West

they slept in, mending clothes or shoes,
reading much-thumbed books, playing cards.
One lay on the riverbank, leisurely washing his linen.

Even the strokes of the field-smithy's hammer slowed
as a mule lifted a last foot to be shod.
The expedition's astronomer fell asleep over his angles.

From the hand of a man writing up the day before,
lest it be lost, the pencil had fallen.
The botanist who, early that morning,

had laid damp papers to dry on the grass
now sagged dimly in his tent.
And the god who, on the eighth day,

created solitude out of the West
turned his face away. The earth turned back
in its stone and grassy dreams

to some already lost hour
when it had only two daughters,
the crag and the clover. Which was I?

This is for my sister the wildflower.

The Landscape of Desire

I. The River of Mercy

In California, where every story is about water
or its lack, I stood in the Sierras and listened

to the River of Mercy pour out what was left of it.
What was there to say in September? A trickle.

I bent even lower—and saw through myself.
How cold the skin of the stream to my stranger's touch.

How lumpy the bed of the Merced, strewn with boulders
the size of boats. Dragged down mountains,

swept up by glaciers, polished the hard way,
then abandoned—rocks, how I loved you that day.

There we were, without knowing it, at the turn
of the "water year," as they say in those parts,

the day the first snowflakes fell even higher up,
in Tuolumne Meadows. Remember, love?

The last day we would spend together.

II. The Valley of Nothing

The valley wanted to be admired.
Though I was driving, I closed my eyes and obliged.

Mountains made of paper, map torn and fading
in the distance it defined—Yosemite wasn't satisfied.

It wanted me to open my eyes. To stop the car.
To stand at the edge of the road at the edge of the world.

The valley disturbed me. On a ropy bridge
over a furious current, my thoughts swayed.

Granite rose like the walls of a room in a dream,
but now I knew why the room was always empty.

Dizzying, such intimacy. I leaned against you, love,
but it wasn't enough. I leaned against a tree.

At my feet fell the world's largest pinecone,
a foot and a half long. I put it under my arm,

like a loaf of bread half hollow, or a prickly doll.
I put it back. It wasn't meant for me.

I closed my eyes and still saw the miles
of scratches that scarred the face of the rock.

Infinity in Fresno

And when I hear the wind
moving and ruffling through these leaves, I set
its voice against that infinite thing, that silence

—LEOPARDI, "L'INFINITO"

We were new friends, the foothills and I—
we kept our distance. I was much closer
to the smog that sank into the valley
and refused to move. But once, thanks to a hint

of wind, the grimy veil lifted. I glimpsed
the staggering rise of mountains
that walled us in from the east. But mostly I sat
in the house of the poet of Van Ness Avenue

and brooded. In the life I'd borrowed
for a season, I pulled a book down
from the highest shelf. *Deep, so deep*
the stillness, Leopardi said.

A scrub jay called, and a freight train,
though not to each other, and not to me.
One tree flagged under the weight
of its lanterns: persimmons signaling

how slow the progress from a state
of ripeness to a state of rot. On the still air
hung the must of grapes laid out to wither
in the raisin capital of the world.

Silence, good neighbor, were you home
the day men came from the county
to flay the eucalyptus in the front yard?
A purely cosmetic operation, I was assured.

I had never drowned in the gorge mirage.

California Aubade

What woke me? A sound I didn't recognize.
Finally I remembered, as if from another life:

rain against a roof. Where was I?
In someone else's house, in someone else's bed.

Slow, sad, expensively green streets
had a rooster as their uncrowned king.

Dawn broke like a ladyfinger over the Fresno Woman's
   Club.
How ladylike the sunrise, thanks to the smog:

a fuzzy pink that one duck flew through,
chasing a rumor of water across the valley.

Had I dreamed the rain? There was no sign of it.
Gardeners arrived from across the tracks

to see each leaf put in its place.

California Elegy

August, and another afternoon
was given to argument, the heat
wilting everything in its path.
Even that scold, the scrub jay,

held his cry. Nothing moved
but three plump chickens out for a stroll.
The cock strutted the empty street,
hens scrabbled in the dry gutter.

Beneath a twisted eucalyptus,
something of darkness stirred.
In the California book of hours,
no longer did leaf-blowers whine,

running the last stray leaf to ground.
Gone were the gardeners in their trucks,
home to smaller plots across the tracks.
In a house not home, I heard the ghost

of a breeze rattle the bones of a wind chime.
The brain surgeon next door pounded
on his fence with a blunt instrument.
Softly a siren throbbed even as it faded.

In the morning I would read in the paper
of a teenage boy from Mexico who
had been knifed outside a bar across town
in the mild small hours of the night.

The Muse at the Door

wanted a word with the poet whose house it was.
"But he's not here," I said.

"Didn't he send you a change of address?"
The heat panted at her heels.

The wind chime said nothing, there being no wind.
She laid an envelope on the poet's pillow.

A drink? She knew where the good wine hid.
She poured herself a glass—

where had she found the Waterford?
She held it to a sticky shaft of sunlight.

I couldn't find a word for that sunstruck red.
She stood over my dirty dishes at the kitchen sink,

gazing out at the garden going to seed on me.
Over the ragged petals of something faded—

a shrimp plant?—there hovered, for an instant,
the word *rubythroat*. And then it was gone.

The Killer Whale of Christmas

Carols caught in the throats of loudspeakers
nailed to trees along the street.
A plywood Spider-Man crouched in a palm tree.
He was all that stood between a Grinch

twice his size and the small Holy Family
finding shelter under an oleander.
Across the street, Santa Claus rode a killer whale,
his elves on dolphins. Oh, to raise a rushlight

and follow a dog out of the hills,
through vineyard and olive grove,
toward some star! But the air was thick
with cars come to make pilgrimage.

In the bare yard of the poet of Van Ness Avenue
I stood, inky shadows chained to my feet.
If time lay down to sleep,
it was in a snowdrift of spun polyester

at the foot of a snowman next door, not here.
Sewn of sailcloth, inflatable,
he would be found, come morning,
shriveled under a thin sheet of dew.

You could hear the age of Augustus rolling on,
an orb, an orange, falling, speechless,
into the dry gutter of December.
Might a shepherd come walking out of an old story?

O my pitiful, prinked millennium!

IV

Experience, its beautiful slag.

—TOMAS TRANSTRÖMER

For a Historian, Dying Young

in memory of Roy Rosenzweig, 1950–2007

I. The History of Landscape

By a pond, a bird,
feathers as starched and white
as nurses' uniforms used to be,

stalked a muddy bank in red high heels.
Down in the muck of Florida
went eight scarlet inches of decurved beak

as if, tired of the clay that passed for food
in the afterlife, an ibis stepped from a frieze
in some young pharaoh's tomb to feed.

Past a pool of ketchup where a french fry fell,
beak and claw left their marks in mud.
Herodotus, father of history, father of lies,

if you're the thin shade under a palm tree
across the water, tell me a story that doesn't end
with my reading in the *Times* today

that Death sits at a desk in Virginia.
Let the tree frogs of Arlington take note.
Let a crow call us to preen our black feathers.

Down leaf-littered sidewalks, down streets that sag
under the names of long-dead presidents—
is that Death the worker making his way in sober suit?

A crumpled page, a fallen leaf, gone too soon.

II. In Their Dream House

Rooms silted up with words,
book laid on book, shelf on shelf,
the sedimentation going back thirty years—

no, everything was gone, walls bare
as blank pages, their parchment scraped
so not even a palimpsest of the past was left.

The historian's desk buried itself in dust,
his computer stopped in its tracks.
Where was his wife, my oldest friend?

I went looking for her in a house
made shifty by dream. In a room I'd never seen,
I found her husband, not yet dead.

He wore the green shirt he'd favored
when he couldn't find the red one—
no, the shirt wore him, the way,

in a church thick with damp, time can turn
a fresco into a cloud of paint
behind which someone, saint or sinner, fades.

How was he, I asked.
Under the lopsided mustache
of an old radical, gone silver,

a ghost of a grin flared and caught.

III. At a Traffic Light

A year ago in Florida, I saw
the blood-blade of a cardinal's wing
cut an afternoon in two:

there was the moment before I thought,
Death, take me instead of him—
and then the rust-feathered female

cleaved leaf back to leaf, my life a lump
still in my hands, not mine to give.
Tonight, in the smallest hour,

what cry woke me?
A small, dark-furred soul lifted on a gold claw?
On great wings, the owl rowed the dark river

of forgetting, rowing home.

The Southern Book of the Dead

I. The Travels of the Dead

were slower in those days. How many weeks
until a Quaker from Philadelphia would stop
at a plantation on the Savannah River?
At night, Bartram wrote, *shortly after our arrival,*

servants came home with horse loads of wild pigeons,
the pigeon of passage having been taken by torchlight,
crowds going out of an evening for the sport of it.
Some took little fascines of fat-pine splinters

for torches; others carried sacks or staves.
Into the swamp they waded, to the place
where the pigeons gathered on low trees in the winter.
The sudden blaze of light blinded the birds,

which, in huge, fluttering numbers, fell to the ground.
Others were beaten off the lowest branches
with sticks, and stuffed into bags. The water,
the flame, and live oaks—on their small, sweet acorns

the birds feasted, having left behind the North.
The scratch of a quill in the underbrush
of an evening, a man dipping the pen's beak
into the dark waters of the inkwell,

the next word bleeding onto the page—
why, that night in the winter of 1776,
did he write the word *servants* instead of *slaves?*

II. The Field Guide of the Dead

was as big as an old family Bible,
but worth more: from deep in the vault
the librarian had to cart it
so I could turn a page of this tombstone.

Each bird was still bright, the gouache unfaded
on the feathers, as if just yesterday
the long-dead artist had sat in a nearby swamp—
sat still enough that he could draw from life.

For so Catesby claimed he had.
But what did *life* mean to a little yellow bird
hung from a branch by a black thread?
Or to the robin on a stump, legs in the air, eye gone dark?

Audubon, was that your ghost I heard riffling the pages
till they whispered *stiff, stiff, stiff*?
So the perfect tinge of its blood-orange breast
glowed like a coal in the fireplace

of your rented Liverpool study?
Yet a lark singing in a cage, a pousse-café in the salon
failed to clear your head of homesickness,
coal smoke in your eyes—Audubon, you old con artist,

you stink of bear grease on your long, wild locks.
Here's a bird you'll recognize.
You caught it better than Catesby did:
the ivory-billed woodpecker, almost extinct.

And how false the next page is,
where a "pigeon of passage" struts carelessly
on the ground, not a single hunter in sight.
On your coonskin cap, you swear

you will capture each feather before it fades.
After all, birds are enough alike,
you can pin another in the same lifelike pose.

To a Hedgehog

Out of the darkness, into the light,
you've tripped: the bulb by the back door
reveals a scrub brush on legs.

Hedgehog, you do not sweep the walk.
You scrape the sky as if to carve
a constellation out of cloud—

as if you, too, have noticed how English overcast
lowers its sooty self to our level.
At the edge of an empire

all trash cans and leaf-litter, you patrol.
You hug the fence in this sad suburb
of history, where rolling into a ball

protects you from everything
but that quadruped come lately, the car.
Some say you can spear fruit

with your five thousand prickles,
some that you suckle milk from cows.
You know better. Teach me

to hear the worm turn under your feet,
and how to crawl under a fallen leaf.
I crouch down so we are brown eye

to brown eye, but too abruptly.
You bristle, my prickly one.
Then, down the long dark alley

of evolution, you continue to wander.

Letter Too Late to Reach Keats as He Awaits Passage to Naples from Gravesend

You'll want a cot that folds to a sofa bed,
a mosquito net of thin gauze.
Fanny may have lined your cap with silk
before you left, but you must have stouter shoes
against the icy marble floors of Italy.

Have you forgotten a pocketknife to eat with?
What of soup, tea, and salt spoons?
A plated teapot, tin teakettle,
phosphorous tinderbox? And pistols, a brace of them.
Where are your napkins (strong, not fine)?

Tea, oatmeal, sago, portable soup—
you must eat, you must make blood.
I would bring you a "soldier's comfort,"
guaranteed as night-lamp, foot warmer, saucepan,
yet little larger than a lady's "ridicule."

The London & Edinburgh Dispensatory
you may recall from your lost days
as a medical student; even one who sketched flowers
instead of taking notes will recognize old friends:
opium, laudanum, blistering salve, some lint.

To carry your own bedding, you should fold it
daily to a size convenient to the carriage,
by way of cushion. Oil of lavender,
four or five drops distributed about a bed
by night, will drive away fleas.

These are the things most requisite
for an invalid, on leaving England.
Pens and penknives, Walkden's ink powder—
but the author of *Travels on the Continent*
has made no mention of paper,

for it can be had there, and better.
Near the Spanish Steps, you will find
an English doctor who believes
there is nothing so grave that riding a horse
in the ruins of Rome will fail to cure it.

Highgate, Suburb of the Dead

Those who died first
slept under the floor of London's churches;
they burrowed
into the churchyards. Outside the old city gate,

those who came later
bedded in overgrown rows. On a summer's day—
sky the gray
of the granite favored here, but heavier—

stones would wait all day
to lose a night's chill. Or for a stranger
to read a few words,
whatever a century of rain hadn't worn away.

In this dormitory of death,
an angel had lost her footing atop a tombstone,
breaking both wings
as she fell. Someone had laid her out

on a toppled marker,
as if in state. Yesterday's newspaper slumped
beside the path,
if it *were* a path, where the weed was lord

of the undergrowth.
Left by the living, cut flowers bowed down.
They prostrated themselves
as in grief. And a blanket of vines crawled up

to comfort or to strangle them.

Summer Recessional

From the last carriage, I watch England go by.
Good-bye, summer, we must go.

Good-bye to that field of barley stubble
we just passed, a blur of worthless gold,

and to that orchard aglow with apples.
The first has fallen, a globe gone sour.

Good-bye, shrunken empire whose sun has set.
Now only the worm of the codling moth will hatch

in the starchy chambers of your decay.
Let it devour whatever sweetness is left.

O empty station, where the train no longer stops!
Had I blinked, I would have missed you.

I'll miss you, too. What are you waiting for?
There is no room in your churchyards for another grave.

O Britannia! Someone's red coat flutters on the edge
of a flag-shaped field scraped down to the dirt.

Shelley Writes to the Minor Poets
Who Come After Him

The journey from Florence to Padua
contained nothing which may not be related
another time. From there, I took a gondola,
finely carpeted and painted black,
with venetian blinds that could be drawn.
That boat must be the most beautiful hearse

in the world, and the most comfortable.
Remember this: without any hint from me,
the gondolier began to speak of a certain *Signor Bee-ron*
who spent great sums of money,
a *giovanotto Inglese* with a *nome stravagante*—
perhaps I had heard of him? No sooner

had I arrived in Venice itself than a waiter, too,
began talking about Lord Byron. At three o'clock
I called at last upon the man himself,
who had just risen. In his own gondola, he took me
to the long, sandy island that defends the city
from the Adriatic, where his horses waited.

As we rode, our conversation consisted
of his wounded feelings and their ancient history,
along with lavish professions of his regard.
We talked of literary matters, too:
his Fourth Canto, he said, is very good,
and he repeated stanzas from memory as evidence.

Should you come this way looking for my ghost,
make your servant take you to good inns,
and pray avoid the Tre Mori at Bologna,

perche vi sono cose inespressibili nei letti.
Do not bother to take the post,
for it is not much faster and very expensive,

and, besides, what is your hurry?
I shall be in no state to receive,
no matter how lavish your letters of introduction.
My heart sits in a jar in Rome, Byron—
always Byron—having saved it from the flames
that dried my drowned bones to ash.

In Limbo

I

Breath turned the frescos to powder, so
    into a sealed antechamber
        we were herded—

whether to lose the chill from our bones
    or to let it seep even deeper,
        in search of the soul,

wasn't clear. We waited. We watched a video
    that explained everything in an Italian
        too musical to follow.

What would Giotto have made of all this?
    I thought of a patch of snow
        I'd seen outside,

hardened, sullied by soot.
    It wouldn't let go of the dirt,
        though this was March,

when the torn cup of a crocus spilled
    the purple of penitence
        on winter's remains.

Each petal laid down by the cold
    was a brushstroke in love
        with raw pigment.

Even as it was rushed onto wet plaster
    to flatter a wealthy donor
        by painting him

in the richest-looking robe,
    saving his soul, the paint
        had begun to fade.

II

Into an old shoebox of a chapel we filed,
    granted fifteen minutes
        to take it all in.

If I stretched out my arms to embrace it,
    I'd touch the walls. The guard
        kept his eye on me.

Don't touch. Don't try to help that angel
    whose coppery wings won't fit
        through the window

of St. Anne's room. Or the man who's tired
    of balancing a model of the chapel
        the size of a dollhouse

on his peeling shoulder. A halo's about to slip.
    Four rivers have burst into flame.
        But the devil,

disguised as an official, papers in his hand,
    merely urges the doomed along.
        How can I not believe

the artist's vision of hell as paperwork?
    The ceiling, sky blazingly blue
        pinned up with stars,

threatens to plunge. I raise my arm to point
    or to push it back into place—
        and then a guard shoos us

back to the poisonous air of the present,
    the eye now come ancient to its work,
    obsessed by its own past.

Grand Opera

Out of breath, here comes our guide,
late, but this is Venice she unlocks a door to.
A fluorescent bulb buzzes and spits
in a sort of purgatory. Where am I?

In a Greyhound bus depot somewhere out West.
Desert of childhood, I would know you
even in a city built on water.
O Grand Canal, my Columbia River!

As if, on the far bank, my father were bent
over his workbench, mending whatever
we'd broken that week. The petty wars
that pass for family happiness

raged upstairs, but in the basement
he listened to opera on the radio.
Long-lost Saturdays! At the top of her lungs,
someone was dying, and not of boredom,

like myself at twelve—no, something grander,
more tedious. How long did it take
for a heart to splinter? The band saw screamed.
Sawdust fell in a heap, and still her voice climbed.

II

We ascended the abrupt back stairs
to Valhalla, Venetian style.
From the high ceiling a chandelier hung,
dripping weakly onto watered silk.

Had we been dead, we might have dined
with long-lost gods in that overdone hall.
Were we heroes of the battles that pass
for family life in king-size myths . . .

had I been the boy in our group,
whose marbled cheek now seemed untouched
by love or anything else—I, who said nothing
when his mother raised her hand to him . . .

I looked around the room saved till last.
The bed sagged under a sunny coverlet of silk.
Where the composer breathed his last,
plastic roses clenched their red fists.

Black Silk

I see myself far off, in a mirror
        that has lost its shine.
                What time is it?
      What year? I stand, naked,
at the sink of a hotel room somewhere,

wringing a cloth. You lie on the bed.
        What are you watching?
            You know my body
      better than I, where it aches,
when it lied. A certain silken gleam:

from even further back, I remember
        a suture of railroad track
           trying to bind
      some siding of civilization
to a tumbleweed, as if that would hold.

It held, scar on my desert of a heart.
        Love, how many years till—
           an ocean away
      and no doctor at hand
in a strange country—you knelt over me

in a rented room and removed a few stitches
        from my skin? You showed
           the awkwardness of one
      who couldn't sew, the tenderness
of one who'd never ripped anything out.

Oblique Epithalamium

I. A Civil Ceremony

In the leaky, wintry light of noon,
a man wrote our names on a marriage certificate.

Across the breadth of a sheet of paper,
in and out of the small plots

that green lines hedged it into,
his fountain pen scratched fishy squiggles,

watery, looking ready to disappear
before he'd filled the blanks in our lives—

but indissoluble, he claimed.
Across a parking lot the gray of the sky,

love, our separate shadows stretched
away from us toward the waiting arms

of the dark. Sunlight scraped from yesterday
rubbed a flake of gold leaf on the fore edge

of the rest of my life. Yours.

II. Self-Portrait with Vanishing Point

Venice, married yet again to the lagoon
that daily tries to drown you,

teach me how life sinks into the future.
Salt has stained whatever it could reach.

Reflecting on the silken sins of your past,
the Grand Canal has turned an unlikely green—

as if a painter's boy mixed pigments wrong
or time proved the yellow fugitive.

The skin of a palazzo has peeled away.
La Serenissima, from each crack and sag,

a past not mine overlooks me. But farther back,
in sepia that sunlight hurried by,

there's a young woman who, if I go closer,
dissolves into daubs without a face:

myself thirty years ago, too young
to turn a corner and see herself today,

going gray on her honeymoon—
Canaletto caught all that.

But here we are, man and wife,
having taken a room. In the distance

of the watercolors hung on three walls,
Vesuvius daintily erupts. From the fourth,

a bowl of fruit in oils serves as witness,
the grapes magmatic, a pear Pompeian,

ashen lump of something left behind.

III. Letter to a Young Man of 1776

William Bartram, 1739–1823

Dear Sir,
          Of the revolution that raged
in the colonies, you found nothing to say.
Thirtysomething, Quaker, son of a man
who, as he readied another cask of plants
to ship from Philadelphia to London,
wondered if you'd ever amount to anything—

he sent you south to collect more species,
a trip not put to paper for a decade,
till what you recalled was leaves, more leaves,
and the odd alligator battle.
How the Romantics loved that flowered prose,
Coleridge slumping over it in a stupor,
Wordsworth taking *Bartram's Travels*
to Germany, the closest he came to the South—

how long had I sat in the twenty-first century
at the old Linnaean Library?
The man I was to meet in London
had not arrived. Instead, I was offered sweets
so British I couldn't name them,
the remains of a Christmas party.

The room grew too grand
for it not to be the eighteenth century,
science still abed with alchemy next door.
Snow hurled its lace against long windows
that searched the parking lot for something

a man could tie someone's name to.
Stiffly on a stiffer chair, I sat,
a North American weed not yet classified.
I didn't recognize myself.

Sixty, married a week, I had just said
the words "my husband" for the first time,
to explain my presence in that hall.
I hadn't taken his name. On my left hand,
the new ring let its weight be felt, warming to me.

The End

Everything soft had been devoured
in the desert of dream.
Something had even taken a tiny bite,
the size of the soul, from a night sky

the same much-laundered blue
as my old school uniform.
Something had risen on dusty wings
after its larval body had feasted.

I chewed on a pencil. Where was a nun
to tell me that pencil and I would burn forever,
or for as long as I stood in the corner,
whichever came first? I sat at a desk

that had grown too small to hold me.
I hadn't done my homework, not for years.
What page were we on? Oh, the blank one
at the end, the one too heavy to turn.

Acknowledgments

Agni: "West of Myself"

Antioch Review: "California Aubade," "Demeter in Winter"

Gettysburg Review: "Bindweed," "California Elegy," "Letter Too Late to Reach Keats as He Awaits Passage to Naples from Gravesend," "The Ruins of Childhood"

Hopkins Review: "Chekhov in English"

Hudson Review: "To a Spoonbill"

Idaho Review: "The Unicorn of Florida"

Kenyon Review: "My First Mermaid," "Summer Recessional"

Literary Imagination: "Shelley Writes to the Minor Poets Who Come After Him," "A Short Pause in the Requiem"

Margie: "Highgate, Suburb of the Dead"

The Nation: "Bitterness"

New Criterion: "Yes"

New England Review: "The End," "Guide to the Dark," "In the Heart of England," "Night School in Florida," "Not Thinking About the Past," "Oblique Epithalamium," "The River of Mercy"

Notre Dame Review: "In Limbo"

OnEarth: "The Southern Book of the Dead"

Paris Review: "The Nightingale of Florida," "To a Hedgehog," "Too Close"

Poetry: "Black Silk," "The Cadillac" (originally published as "The Cadillac of the Dead"), "Dances of 1964"

Raritan: "After the Hurricane," "The Clock in the Heart," "Dream with Basement," "For a Historian, Dying Young," "Grand Opera"

River City: "A Short History of the West," "Still Life with Hurricane"

Smartish Pace: "Infinity in Fresno"

Southern Review: "One Sunday out West"

Southwest Review: "Domestic Manners of the Americans," "The Landscape of Desire," "Self-Portrait with Vanishing Point"

TriQuarterly: "Death Takes a Holiday," "The Middle of Nowhere," "Persephone on the Way to Hell," "Preserves"

Washington Square: "After the Fall: Eve in Florida"

Yale Review: "The Killer Whale of Christmas," "The Muse at the Door"

DEBORA GREGER is the author of eight previous books of poems. She has won, among other honors, the Grolier Prize, the Discovery/*The Nation* Award, an Award in Literature from the American Academy of Arts and Letters, and grants from the Guggenheim Foundation and the National Endowment for the Arts. She lives in Florida and in Cambridge, England.

Penguin Poets

JOHN ASHBERY
Selected Poems
Self-Portrait in a Convex
  Mirror

TED BERRIGAN
The Sonnets

LAUREN BERRY
The Lifting Dress

JOE BONOMO
Installations

PHILIP BOOTH
Selves

JULIANNE BUCHSBAUM
The Apothecary's Heir

JIM CARROLL
Fear of Dreaming:
  The Selected Poems
Living at the Movies
Void of Course

ALISON HAWTHORNE DEMING
Genius Loci
Rope

CARL DENNIS
Callings
New and Selected Poems
  1974-2004
Practical Gods
Ranking the Wishes
Unknown Friends

DIANE DI PRIMA
Loba

STUART DISCHELL
Backwards Days
Dig Safe

STEPHEN DOBYNS
Velocities: New and Selected
  Poems, 1966-1992

EDWARD DORN
Way More West: New and
  Selected Poems

ROGER FANNING
The Middle Ages

ADAM FOULDS
The Broken Word

CARRIE FOUNTAIN
Burn Lake

AMY GERSTLER
Crown of Weeds:
  Poems
Dearest Creature
Ghost Girl
Medicine
Nerve Storm

EUGENE GLORIA
Drivers at the Short-Time
  Motel
Hoodlum Birds
My Favorite Warlord

DEBORA GREGER
By Herself
Desert Fathers, Uranium
  Daughters
God
Men, Women, and Ghosts
Western Art

TERRANCE HAYES
Hip Logic
Lighthead
Wind in a Box

ROBERT HUNTER
Sentinel and Other Poems

MARY KARR
Viper Rum

WILLIAM KECKLER
Sanskrit of the Body

JACK KEROUAC
Book of Sketches
Book of Blues
Book of Haikus

JOANNA KLINK
Circadian
Raptus

JOANNE KYGER
As Ever: Selected Poems

ANN LAUTERBACH
Hum
If in Time: Selected Poems,
  1975–2000
On a Stair
Or to Begin Again

CORINNE LEE
PYX

PHILLIS LEVIN
May Day
Mercury

WILLIAM LOGAN
Macbeth in Venice
Madame X
Strange Flesh
The Whispering Gallery

ADRIAN MATEJKA
Mixology

MICHAEL MCCLURE
Huge Dreams: San Francisco
  and Beat Poems

DAVID MELTZER
David's Copy: The Selected
  Poems of David Meltzer

ROBERT MORGAN
Terroir

CAROL MUSKE-DUKES
An Octave above Thunder
Red Trousseau
Twin Cities

ALICE NOTLEY
Culture of One
The Descent of Alette
Disobedience
In the Pines
Mysteries of Small Houses

LAWRENCE RAAB
The History of Forgetting
Visible Signs: New and
  Selected Poems

BARBARA RAS
The Last Skin
One Hidden Stuff

MICHAEL ROBBINS
Alien vs. Predator

PATTIANN ROGERS
Generations
Wayfare

WILLIAM STOBB
Absentia
Nervous Systems

TRYFON TOLIDES
An Almost Pure Empty
  Walking

ANNE WALDMAN
Kill or Cure
Manatee/Humanity
Structure of the World
  Compared to a Bubble

JAMES WELCH
Riding the Earthboy 40

PHILIP WHALEN
Overtime: Selected Poems

ROBERT WRIGLEY
Beautiful Country
Earthly Meditations: New
  and Selected Poems
Lives of the Animals
Reign of Snakes

MARK YAKICH
The Importance of Peeling
  Potatoes in Ukraine
Unrelated Individuals
  Forming a Group Waiting
  to Cross

JOHN YAU
Borrowed Love Poems
Paradiso Diaspora